Who on earth is the Holy Spirt?

And other questions about who he is and what he does

Tim Chester &
Christopher de la Hoyde

Who on earth is the Holy Spirit?
And other questions about who he is and what he does
Part of the *Questions Christians Ask* series

Published by
The Good Book Company
Tel (UK): 0333 123 0880
Tel (North America): (1) 866 244 2165
International: +44 (0) 208 942 0880
Email (UK): admin@thegoodbook.co.uk
Email (North America): sales@thegoodbook.com

Websites
UK & Europe: www.thegoodbook.co.uk
North America: www.thegoodbook.com
Australia: www.thegoodbook.com.au
New Zealand: www.thegoodbook.co.nz

ISBN: 9781908762320 | Printed in the UK

Design by André Parker

Contents

Introduction **5**

1 **The Spirit of life** **11**
Why is the Spirit sometimes called "the Holy Ghost"? **12**
Did believers in the Old Testament have the Holy Spirit? **18**
Should Christians look to receive the Holy Spirit after their conversion? **24**

2 **The Spirit of God** **25**
What does it mean to be filled with the Spirit? **30**

3 **The Spirit of love** **39**
Is the Spirit a person or a force? **42**
Should we pray to the Spirit? **53**

4 **The Spirit of truth** **55**
What is the gift of prophecy and is it for today? **64**

5 **The Spirit of power** **67**
Should we expect Pentecost to be repeated? **73**
Are miraculous gifts for today? **77**

Introduction

Gary was confused. He'd been a believer for a little while. He was growing in his knowledge of Jesus, and had got stuck in with a local church. But he was feeling unsettled.

He'd been told soon after he became a Christian that the Holy Spirit came to live in all believers. But what he heard people saying about the Holy Spirit confused him: things like, "the Spirit really helped me", or "I feel like the Spirit's really putting his finger on this thing in my life".

And sometimes people in prayer meetings encouraged those present to pray "as the Spirit leads you".

As he read his Bible, he kept coming across phrases that puzzled him, like "praying in the Spirit", having "joy in the Spirit" and being "filled with the Spirit".

The thing was, he wasn't sure he knew what any of that meant, or if he'd ever experienced any of that. Did he really have the Holy Spirit at all then? For that matter, *who on earth is the Holy Spirit?*

Do you ever feel like Gary? Many people are confused about the Holy Spirit—who he is, what he does, what he's like and what we should expect from him. And many people feel uneasy when talking about him.

In Galatians 3 v 2-5 Paul says:

> Let me ask you this one question: Did you receive the Holy Spirit by obeying the law of Moses? Of course not! You received the Spirit because you believed the message you heard about Christ. How foolish can you be? After starting your Christian lives in the Spirit, why are you now trying to become perfect by your own human effort? Have you experienced so much for nothing? Surely it was not in vain, was it? I ask you again, does God give you the Holy Spirit and work miracles among you because you obey the law? Of course not! It is because you believe the message you heard about Christ. *(New Living Translation)*

Paul's point here is very clear: *You began the Christian life by faith and in the Spirit. So why switch to living by law?* All the blessings you have received, you have received by faith and by the Spirit. So why switch to an alternative way of living?

But this argument only works if the Spirit is a noticeable experience. Verse 2 doesn't work if the Galatians aren't sure whether they've received the Spirit. Paul is appealing to their *experience*. You've all experienced the life of the Spirit, says Paul. How did that experience come about? By law or by faith? It was by faith. What's assumed is that *they have all experienced the Spirit.* The Spirit's work is not an unseen or unfelt reality.

This means you can't experience the Holy Spirit without noticing!

Which leaves us with an important question: *Have I actually experienced the Holy Spirit? And what does it actually look like, or feel like to experience the Holy Spirit?*

Francis Schaeffer once said:

> *Supposing we had awakened today to find everything concerning the Holy Spirit and prayer removed from the Bible ... What difference would it make practically between the way we worked yesterday and the way we would work today, and tomorrow? What difference would it make in the majority of Christians' practical work and plans? ... Isn't much work done by human talent, energy, and clever ideas? Where does the supernatural power of God have a real place?*[1]

Francis Chan poses a similar challenge:

> *If you or I had never been to a church and had read only the Old and New Testaments, we would have significant expectations of the Holy Spirit in our lives ... If we read and believed these accounts, we would expect a great deal of the Holy Spirit ... We would expect our new life with the*

---

1 Cited in Edith Schaeffer, **L'Abri,** Tyndale, 1969, 64-65.

Holy Spirit to look radically different from our old life without him.[1]

Are we missing out on the fulness of life in the Spirit?

Our aim in this book is twofold.

Reassurance

We want to reassure you. For some of us, life in the Spirit sounds intimidating. It seems to speak of an experience that's not ours. We think of people having visions or intense emotions and it all seems a long way from the mundane realities of our lives. As we describe the experience of life in the Spirit in these pages, we hope we'll describe *your* experience. The life in the Spirit is the life you lead—not fully, not perfectly, but you'll recognise the signs of the Spirit's work in your own life.

Expectation

But we also want you to be much more aware of the *work* of the Spirit. In recent years discussions about the the Holy Spirit have often focused on a narrow range of issues. We'll touch on some of these. But we want the focus to be on what we think are the *central* activities of the Spirit.

We want to raise your expectation of the Spirit's work in your life. When you pray, we want you to expect the Spirit to work miracles. When you talk about Jesus, we want you to expect the Spirit to create faith in people's

---

1 Francis Chan, **The Forgotten God: Reversing Our Tragic Neglect of the Holy Spirit,** David C. Cook, 2009, 30-31.

hearts. When you read God's word, we want you to expect the Spirit to create intimacy with the Father. When you're tempted, we want you to expect the Spirit to give you alternative desires.

In your daily life, we want you to expect the Spirit to show you how you can serve others in love. We want you to be able to appeal to the experience of the Spirit as Paul does in Galatians 3 v 2-5.

Chapter 1

The Spirit of life

Jane was really pleased about her new church. She was particularly excited about their homeless ministry. And she was so grateful that after the first meeting she attended, she'd been invited back for a meal with a lovely group of people. But she'd woken the next day with a strange feeling, a feeling of insecurity. Towards the end of the afternoon, one of the girls had asked her whether she had the Spirit. "Yes," she said, "I think so". But it struck her that "I think so" perhaps wasn't a great answer. She thought she had the Spirit. But now she wasn't so sure. *What did having the Spirit look like?*

Maybe you can relate to Jane. You've been told you have the Spirit. But when you hear people talking about the Spirit's work in their lives, you begin to wonder if you really do. Let's start by looking at Titus 3 v 3-7:

> **At one time we too were foolish, disobedient, deceived and enslaved by all kinds of passions**

> and pleasures. We lived in malice and envy, being hated and hating one another. But when the kindness and love of God our Saviour appeared, he saved us, not because of righteous things we had done, but because of his mercy. He saved us through the washing of rebirth and renewal by the Holy Spirit, whom he poured out on us generously through Jesus Christ our Saviour, so that, having been justified by his grace, we might become heirs having the hope of eternal life.
>
> *Titus 3 v 3-7*

Everything God does, he does as Father, Son and Spirit. God is a tri-unity or trinity, a unity of three persons. All three members of the Trinity work together in everything God does. And there's no exception here. Who rescues sinners? Is it the Father, the Son or the Spirit? It's all three together!

The Father started it all off. The plan of salvation was initiated by his love. It's his kindness that has appeared.

Why is the Spirit sometimes called "the Holy Ghost"?

When the early translators of the Bible into English used the word "ghost", it didn't just mean (as it does today) spooky things that haunt old houses. It meant what we now mean by the word "spirit". In old English the word for "spirit" is "gast". The equivalent word in German ("geist") still has the broader sense, as the word *zeitgeist* (spirit of the times) shows.

And he did it all "through Jesus Christ our Saviour". But it's the Spirit who completes the work. It's the Spirit who brings about new life in us. Verse 5 says: "He saved us through the washing of rebirth and renewal by the Holy Spirit, whom he poured out on us generously through Jesus Christ our Saviour."

The Spirit gives spiritual life to spiritually dead people

We were "dead" in our sins. That's how Paul puts it in Ephesians 2 v 1. What does that mean? We're all in a process of physical decay that ends in death. One day our bodies will return to dust. But we're not just physically dying. We were also *spiritually dead.* We were unable to respond to God in any way.

Last year my (Chris's) children, who were six, four and two at the time, found a dead bird in the garden. We'd been reading about Jesus raising Lazarus from the dead, so we decided to do a little experiment. We shouted instructions at the bird as loudly as we could to see if we could make it do things. "Get up!" shouted Zac, the two-year-old, at the top of his voice. Nothing. "Fly!" screamed Jethro. "Squawk!" screeched Elsa. *Nothing.* We could shout as loud as we wanted. But the bird was dead. It couldn't hear us. It couldn't respond to us at all.

That's how each of us was towards God. As Paul puts it in Titus 3 v 3, we were "foolish, disobedient, deceived and enslaved by all kinds of passions". Jesus "gave himself for us to redeem us from all wickedness" (Titus 2 v 14). But you were enslaved to your sin, your heart was hard, you were unable to respond with faith. The death of Jesus was useless to you.

What's changed? Why do you now trust Jesus? Because the day came when:

> God saved [you] through the washing of rebirth and renewal by the Holy Spirit, whom he poured out on [you] generously through Jesus Christ our Saviour." *Titus 3 v 5-6*

Through the Spirit, God gave you a new heart, a new life, new desires and new loves. The Holy Spirit has made you spiritually alive. As a result, you have recognised the beauty of Jesus and the power of his work, and so you have turned to him in faith.

Hannah was one of my wife's work colleagues. She used to love spending time with our congregation. But she found the gospel message just plain weird!

We did some Bible studies with her over the summer and she kept looking at us in astonishment. We would read about Jesus walking on water, rising from the dead and ascending into heaven. "You really believe all of this?" she would ask.

Later she told us that what we believed sounded crazy, yet she kept telling herself: "They seem like sensible people who're able to hold down jobs". Then one day a member of our community challenged her. "Don't wait until all your questions have been answered," she said. "Just ask yourself whether you can trust Jesus."

Hannah went home and she describes how she was sitting on the floor in her front room when suddenly she knew it was all true. In that moment she became a Christian.

What happened as she sat on her living room floor?

The Holy Spirit came on her. There was no shining light or audible voice. But the Holy Spirit came to give her faith in Jesus.

This is what Jesus means when he says: "I tell you the truth, no-one can see the kingdom of God unless he is born again" (John 3 v 3). He explains: "Flesh gives birth to flesh, but the Spirit gives birth to spirit" (John 3 v 6). In other words, the Spirit gives us spiritual life. It's like being born again into a new life.

The theological word for this new birth is "regeneration" or "rebirth". And without regeneration we just *can't see* God's kingdom. We can hear all the facts, but we don't see Christ as our King and Saviour. To see it, to get it, to grasp it we need the Holy Spirit to do his work in us.

Implications

What does this life-giving work of the Spirit mean for us? First, it means ***salvation is God's work from beginning to end***. It's all by his grace. The Father planned it in his kindness. The Son bought it in his love. And the Spirit brought it home to our hard, lifeless hearts through his amazing grace. God doesn't say: "I've done this much. Now you can do the rest yourself." He does it all, from first to last.

Second, it means that ***even your faith is a gift from God.*** "It is by grace you have been saved, through faith—and this is not from yourselves, it is the gift of

God." (Ephesians 2 v 8) You didn't put your faith in Jesus because you were wise or clever. The only reason you trust Christ is because God gave you new life and worked faith in your heart. And that's the work of the Holy Spirit. God gave his Son to rescue us from his judgment. God gives his Spirit to move us to take hold of the rescue his Son has achieved.

The sixteenth-century reformer, John Calvin puts it like this:

> *As long as Christ remains outside of us, and we are separated from him, all that he has suffered and done for the salvation of the human race remains useless and of no value to us.*

Calvin says that to benefit from what Christ has achieved, we need to be united to him. Christ is like a treasure chest, where all of the good things he has won on the cross are stored. If we want to enjoy those good things, then we must be united with Christ. And Calvin is clear that "we obtain this by faith". However, as Calvin says, "not all indiscriminately embrace that communion with Christ which is offered through the gospel". Without God's intervention we are dead in our sins. So it is only through "the secret energy of the Spirit ... by which we come to enjoy Christ and all his benefits."[1] The Spirit unites us with Christ through faith.

Third, the Spirit's work means that ***every Christian has been transformed by the Spirit***. Paul says:

---

1 John Calvin, **Institutes of the Christian Religion**, Westminster John Knox Press, 1960, 3.1.1.

> If anyone does not have the Spirit of Christ, he does not belong to Christ. But if Christ is in you, your body is dead because of sin, yet your spirit is alive because of righteousness. *Romans 8 v 9-10*

In other words, if you don't have the Spirit then you can't be a Christian. But if you are a Christian then you have the Spirit. You must have! Because only the Spirit gives spiritual life. The sure sign of the Spirit's work in someone's life is faith in Christ.

Look how emphatic Paul is about this point:

> He saved us through the washing of rebirth and renewal by the Holy Spirit, whom he has poured out on us generously through Jesus Christ our Saviour.
> *Titus 3 v 5-6*

God hasn't just sent his Spirit to influence you occasionally. He's poured the Spirit out generously on you. You're drenched in the Spirit! However small or weak you may feel as a Christian, you have an exciting future ahead of you because God the Spirit himself lives in you in all his fulness.

The Spirit gives life in creation

The Nicene Creed says the Spirit is "the giver of life." We've seen how the Spirit gives life to spiritually dead people. But the Spirit is also the giver of life in the rest of creation.

> The earth was formless and empty, darkness was

Did believers in the Old Testament have the Holy Spirit?

In the Old Testament, God's power came on individuals to equip them to lead or rescue God's people. But this only happened to a few of them. The Old Testament promises a day when all of God's people will receive God's Spirit so they can know him for themselves (Isaiah 32 v 15; Jeremiah 31 v 33-34; Ezekiel 36 v 24-27; 39 v 29). The New Testament says this promise was fulfilled at Pentecost (Acts 2 v 17-18, 33, 38; Galatians 3 v 14).

But we've seen that, to have faith at all, the Spirit needs to open our eyes. If most Old Testament believers didn't have the Spirit, how could they be believers? Were they given new birth by the Spirit? Christians have answered this question is different ways.[1]

- Old Testament believers were born again and in-dwelt by the Holy Spirit (John Owen, B. B. Warfield, Sinclair Ferguson).
- Old Testament believers were born again and in-dwelt by the Holy Spirit, but New Testament believers experience this in a greater way (Augustine, John Calvin, Wayne Grudem).
- Old Testament believers were regenerate, but not in-dwelt by the Holy Spirit (J. I. Packer, Bruce Ware).
- Old Testament believers were not born again, but the Spirit did give them faith in God's promises. The Spirit acted on them, but did not fill them (Martin Luther, Don Carson, Michael Green).

---

1 See James Hamilton, **Were Old Testament Believers Indwelt by the Holy Spirit?** Themelios 30.1 (September 2004), 12-22.

> over the surface of the deep, and the Spirit of God was hovering over the waters. *Genesis 1 v 2*

The Spirit was at work in creation bringing order out of disorder. In Genesis 6 – 8 God "unmakes" the world in judgment against humanity's sin. At creation he separated the waters and the land, but now the waters swallow up the land again in a great flood.

Then in Genesis 8 v 1 we read:

> God remembered Noah and all the wild animals and the livestock that were with him in the ark, and he sent a wind over the earth, and the waters receded.

The word for "wind" here (the Hebrew word is *ruach*) is the same word used for the Spirit of God in Genesis 1. As God remakes his world after judgment, it's the Spirit who again tames the waters. We see this again in the story of Israel's rescue from Egypt:

> Moses stretched out his hand over the sea, and all that night the LORD drove the sea back with a strong east wind and turned it into dry land. The waters were divided, and the Israelites went through the sea on dry ground, with a wall of water on their right and on their left.
>
> *Exodus 14 v 21-22*

The Spirit descends as a wind, hovers over waters and separates them to create dry land. The Spirit fashions the space in which God creates or rescues people. Whenever we see beauty in creation, we see evidence of the Spirit's work.

But the Spirit doesn't just shape creation. He breathes life into it. The word "Spirit" can mean "breath" as well as "wind". Genesis 2 v 7 says: "The LORD God formed the man from the dust of the ground and breathed into his nostrils the breath of life, and the man became a living being." In Genesis 7 v 22 having "the breath of life in its nostrils" is another way of talking about the life of living creatures.

Job 33 v 4 says: "The Spirit of God has made me; the breath of the Almighty gives me life." So the Spirit or breath of God gives life to everything that has life in creation. Wherever we see life in creation, we see evidence of the Spirit's work.

Giving life now

But the Spirit's life-giving work wasn't just at the beginning. After Adam and Eve disobeyed God, God cursed creation and death entered the world. That's why we live in a world of sickness and disasters. But God remains committed to his creation. Psalm 104 praises God not only for making everything in creation (v 5-9), but also for sustaining it (v 10-30). As the psalm moves towards its concluding call to praise, we read:

> All creatures look to you
>   to give them their food at the proper time ...
> when you take away their breath,
>   they die and return to the dust.
> When you send your Spirit,

they are created,
and you renew the face of the ground.

Psalm 104 v 27-30

The Spirit who breathed life into lifeless creation continues to breathe life into decaying creation. Graham Tomlin puts it like this:

> *After the fall, once the creation has been subjected to frustration, the Spirit has another, additional function: to oppose the spirit of death and destruction, all that seeks to unravel God's good purposes for the world, and instead to renew a decaying world.'*[1]

The Spirit gives a foretaste of life in the new creation

The Spirit who gives life to creation also gives Christians a foretaste of life in the new creation. My mother used to spend hours sewing name-tags into my school clothes. She knew that otherwise I'd lose them—or have them stolen! ***The Spirit is God's seal on us.*** He is like God's name tag, making sure we're his until the day of glory.

In Ephesians 1 v 13 Paul says: "When you believed, you were marked in him with a seal, the promised Holy Spirit." Cattle and slaves were branded with a seal to show who was their owner and protect them from theft.

---

1 Graham Tomlin, **The Prodigal Spirit: The Trinity, the Church and the Future of the World**, St Paul's Theological Centre, 2011, 39.

The Holy Spirit is God's mark of ownership on us. He's the sign that God will protect us as his own until the day of redemption. The Spirit makes us confident that we are part of God's family.

In verse 14 Paul changes the picture. He describes the Spirit as "a deposit guaranteeing our inheritance until the redemption of those who are God's possession—to the praise of his glory".

If you pay a deposit for something, you get a slip of paper saying it's yours. It can't be sold to anyone else. It guarantees that it belongs to you—even though you've not received it yet. The Holy Spirit is God's deposit to us, the pledge that God will deliver our heavenly inheritance.

But the Spirit is more than a deposit. Paul uses a word that also means *a first instalment.* The deposit comes in the form of a first instalment. The Spirit gives us something of the reality of the new creation in the present—even if it is only a fraction of what's to come. In Romans 8 v 23 Paul describes what we have now as the "firstfruits of the Spirit". We've been given a part of what's in store!

Why? ***As a guarantee that it really is coming!***

When a man gives a woman an engagement ring, it's a pledge that he'll marry her. The Spirit is a pledge of our inheritance. But he's more than this. An engagement ring isn't a foretaste of marriage. So the Spirit is more like a lover's kiss—he's both a pledge and a foretaste of marriage. Or the gift of the Spirit is like being allowed into the kitchen to have a little taste of the wonderful banquet that's being prepared. The blessings of the Spirit are a foretaste of God's wonderful banquet. Through the Spirit we already enjoy something of the life of heaven in the Christian community.

But what exactly does that look and feel like? That's what we'll be exploring in the rest of this book.

Should Christians look to receive the Holy Spirit after their conversion?

This is an issue about which Christians disagree. In 1 Corinthians 12 v 13 Paul speaks of being "baptised by one Spirit". Pentecostal and some charismatic Christians believe we should look for a second experience of being "baptised in the Spirit" after we've become a Christian. And many Christians can point to a time in their lives when they became aware of the work of the Spirit in a new way.

Other Christians believe "baptism in the Spirit" is simply one of the ways the Bible describes the inner transformation or "regeneration" the Spirit brings. This transformation is what leads to faith in Christ—so by definition every Christian has received the Holy Spirit.

What is clear is that without the Holy Spirit *you can't become a Christian.* This isn't to discount the experiences people have had, but it *does* mean they're not necessarily the pattern for every believer.

Whatever you think about this issue, we can all ask God for a greater experience of the Spirit's work in our lives. That work may take place through dramatic experiences or it may take place through a gradual growth.

Chapter 2

The Spirit of God

John was lonely. He'd resisted turning to Jesus for years, worried about the consequences. But just eighteen months ago he'd finally seen that his life was a mess and there wasn't anything he could do about it.

He couldn't be the husband he wanted to be, the friend he wanted to be, or even the employee he wanted to be. He'd turned to Jesus in repentance and faith. And things were great for a while. His struggles with anger seemed to subside. He found himself able to take a knock more easily.

But then his wife left him for someone else, saying it was because he wasn't the man she'd married anymore. Then he lost the job he'd had ever since he'd left school and all the friends who came with it. He had to leave his house because he couldn't afford the rent. And he had to get rid of his beloved car.

John thought that being a Christian would sort his life out, make it all work better. But the opposite seemed to have happened. He had a supportive church family around him, but when he got back to his rented room in the evening, John couldn't deny it. He felt as if he was completely alone.

Have you ever felt like John?

God living with his people: the story of the Bible

At its heart, the Bible is the story of God coming to live with his people. That's how it begins. God is living with his people, walking in the garden in the cool of the day (Genesis 3 v 8). But then disaster strikes. Deceived by the serpent, Adam and Eve rebel against God. They're thrown out of the garden and barred from God's presence. Sinful people cannot live in the presence of a holy God.

But all is not lost. In the book of Exodus God rescues his chosen people from slavery in Egypt. But he's not just rescuing them *from* slavery. He's rescuing them *for* a relationship with himself. The climax of the book of Exodus comes when the glory of God fills the tabernacle. Once again God lives among his people in all his glory.

And yet there's a problem. The people are still sinful and God is still holy. So they can't actually enter into his presence. God lives among his people. But they can't come near to him: God said that he would "break out against" them (Exodus 19 v 22; 33 v 5) if they tried.

The book of Leviticus sets out a complex system of cleanliness and rituals to illustrate this truth. It describes various sacrifices by which people could approach God. The centrepiece of this system was the Day of Atonement. On that day (and that day alone) the high priest (and the high priest alone) could enter the heart of the tabernacle, the Most Holy Place (Holy of Holies), the symbol of God's holy presence, to make atonement for the people's sin through sacrifice. Any move outside this system exposed sinful people to judgment—as Nadab and Abihu, the sons of Aaron, discovered when they offered "unauthorised fire" (see Numbers 3 v 2-4).

But by the time the prophet Ezekiel arrived on the scene several centuries later, everything had gone wrong. Because of their sin, God's people had been deported from the land God gave to them. And in Ezekiel 10 the prophet saw a vision of God's glory leaving the temple. A holy God cannot live among a rebellious people.

This, however, is not the end of the story. In the final chapters of the book of Ezekiel, God promised a time when he would pour out his Spirit on his people in a brand new way (36 v 27; 39 v 29). He promises to restore his people to himself and move them to obey his commandments. Not only this, God gave Ezekiel a breathtaking vision: a new temple-city. But Ezekiel leaves the highpoint of the vision until the very last final verse: "The name of the city from that day shall be: 'The LORD is there'." (Ezekiel 48 v 35).

After 70 years the people returned to the land and the temple was rebuilt. But it was a pale shadow of the old temple, let alone Ezekiel's vision of a new temple! God's people remained every bit as wayward as before. Ezekiel's prophecy had not come true.

Until one day 400 years later a man from Nazareth appears near the Jordan River. The apostle John calls this man "the Word" of God (John 1 v 1). He says:

> The Word became flesh and made his dwelling among us. We have seen his glory, the glory of the one and only Son, who came from the Father, full of grace and truth. *John 1 v 14*

God has come to live among his people in all of his glory, and he has done so by becoming a man. Jesus himself is the place where God now dwells among his people (see John 2 v 19-21).

Yet still the story hasn't reached its conclusion. Jesus died, rose and ascended to be with his Father. He no longer lives physically among his people. The story won't be complete until Jesus comes back and God makes his dwelling-place among his people for ever (Revelation 21 v 1-3).

But as Jesus went to be with his Father, he promised: "Surely I am with you always, to the very end of the age" (Matthew 28 v 20). He promises them a little foretaste of heaven. Through the death and resurrection of Jesus, God can live with people—not just symbolically in the form of a temple, but personally.

How does Jesus do that? How does he come to live with believers? He keeps his promise at Pentecost. Jesus himself doesn't come physically—not yet. Instead, the Spirit makes Christ present in believers.

God's aim throughout the Bible story is to make a people among whom he will live. And it's the Spirit who brings about these purposes in our lives. In the Old Testament the temple was the symbol of God's presence with his people. The New Testament describes the church as God's temple; we are now the place on earth where God dwells:

> In [Christ] the whole building is joined together and rises to become a holy temple in the Lord. And in him you too are being built together to become a dwelling in which God lives by his Spirit. *Ephesians 2 v 21-22*

God living with his people: the glory of the Spirit's work

The night before his death, Jesus said to his disciples:

> ...but now I am going to him who sent me. None of you asks me, "Where are you going?" Rather, you are filled with grief because I have said these things. But very truly I tell you, it is for your good that I am going away. Unless I go away, the Advocate will not come to you; but if I go, I will send him to you. *John 16 v 5-7*

Imagine the disciples' bewilderment. Here was their master and friend breaking the news that he's leaving them. But Jesus says it's actually *better* for them if he goes away. They must have felt like a wife who comes home to find a note from her husband saying it's best for everyone if he leaves her. *How could that be for their good?*

The answer is that Jesus will send the Advocate (Counsellor), the Holy Spirit, to replace him. The Holy Spirit living in you is better than Jesus himself walking around at your side. Do you believe that? I know I often don't!

Think of it like this. The disciples had spent three years with Jesus. Day after day they saw him, heard him,

What does it mean to be filled with the Spirit?

In Ephesians 5 v 18 Paul says: "Do not get drunk on wine, which leads to debauchery. Instead, be filled with the Spirit." What does it mean to be filled with the Spirit? The verb "be filled" means "go on being filled". This is not a one-off experience, but a Spirit-filled life. But what does this involve? The key is to realise that Paul isn't talking to individuals, but to a church. He's not telling me to be Spirit-filled. He's telling my church to be filled with the Spirit! How do we get to be like that? Paul goes on to list four activities that explain what it means to be filled with the Spirit. What he says more literally in Ephesians 5 v 19-21 is:

> **Be continuously filled with the Spirit: speaking to one another with psalms, hymns and spiritual songs; singing and making music in your heart to the Lord; always giving thanks to God the Father for everything, in the name of our Lord Jesus Christ; submitting to one another out of reverence for Christ.**

Is your church a place where people encourage one another with the truth of the gospel? Do people sing Christ's praise with excitement? Are people bursting with gratitude to God for Jesus, even in the hard times? Are people so taken up with the glory of Jesus that they love to serve others? If so, then it's a Spirit-filled church.

But notice that Paul commands us to be filled with the Spirit. How do we do that? How do we become touched him. Yet still they were blind to who he was. In the end they denied him and deserted him. But through the work of the Spirit, Jesus lives in us. *And Jesus living in us is even better than Jesus living near us.* The Spirit transformed the disciples from doubting deserters into bold witnesses.

Through the Spirit, Christ is present with all believers all of the time (Romans 8 v 9-10). When things are tough, when we sin, when we're sinned against, when people reject us—Christ is present in us. Through the Spirit, Christ himself lives in us and whispers his word of hope into our hearts.

As we've seen, the climax of the prophecy of Ezekiel is the declaration of the name of the new city: "THE LORD IS THERE" (Ezekiel 48 v 35). Those words find an echo in the declaration of 1 Corinthians 14 v 24: *"God is really among you!"* In the Spirit-filled church of the new covenant, God is really there. But in 1 Corinthians 14 it's not a prophet who makes this announcement. It's an unbeliever! When God is present with his people

or remain a Spirit-filled church? Don't wait for others or complain about your church. Be part of the solution. Talk to others about Jesus. Remind one another of the gospel through songs that excite our affections. Sing Christ's praises with enthusiasm and energy. Stop moaning or complaining and instead be intentional about giving thanks to God together. Put other people first. And pray that, as you do that, the Spirit will fire people's hearts with love for Christ.

through his Spirit, the world takes note. The life of a Spirit-filled Christian community shows off the gospel.

Acts 2 v 42-47 describes the first Spirit-filled church. What was its impact? "The Lord added to their number daily those who were being saved." A Spirit-filled church defies natural explanation. Why? Because something supernatural needs a supernatural explanation. And that explanation is the gospel. It's the good news that Christ has died and risen so we can be reconciled with God, and now God has come to dwell among us in the person of his Spirit: *God is really among you!*

But what does it mean to have God live in us by his Spirit?

1. The Spirit sets us apart for God

One answer is that the Spirit makes us holy. He is, after all, the *Holy* Spirit, the Spirit of holiness. The Bible calls this "sanctification", which means "being made holy". Sanctification involves two connected things. The first is sometimes called "definitive sanctification".

Our garden is littered with plant pots. They get used for all sorts of things: as goalposts, hats and even as emergency potties when the bathroom is in use. But imagine that one day my wife chooses one of those plant pots to grow strawberries. She carefully fills it with compost and beds in the strawberry plants. Every day she feeds and waters the pot. Now it's set apart for her use. It's special. The boys and I can't use it as a goalpost any more. Nobody can wee in it or use it as a hat. It's my wife's special plant pot set apart for her special use.

That's what "definitive sanctification" is. It's what

happens when God's Spirit comes and makes his home in us. God sets us apart for his special use.

> Don't you know that you yourselves are God's temple and that God's Spirit lives among you? If anyone destroys God's temple, God will destroy that person; for God's temple is sacred, and you together are that temple.
>
> *1 Corinthians 3 v 16-17*

The Old Testament temple was a holy place, God's place. You couldn't do whatever you wanted there. You had to be ceremonially clean to enter it. It was a place that was set apart as God's space. But now, says Paul, the church is God's temple. It's sacred (or holy) to God. What makes us God's holy temple? The fact that God's Spirit lives among us. The Spirit sets us apart as God's holy people.

In 1 Corinthians 6 v 18-20 Paul also says that *individual believers* are temples of the Holy Spirit:

> Flee from sexual immorality ... Do you not know that your bodies are temples of the Holy Spirit, who is in you, whom you have received from God? You are not your own; you were bought at a price. Therefore honour God with your bodies.

You're set apart for God. So you can't just live however you want. You're to live a holy life because your life belongs to God now!

2. The Spirit makes us more like Jesus

But there's a problem. We might be holy—set apart for God. But we don't live holy lives. We sin in a hundred different ways every day.

The good news is that the Spirit doesn't just set us apart as holy. ***He also changes us.*** Over the course of our lives, he transforms us so that we become the holy people God has called us to be. This process is sometimes called "progressive sanctification".

Before we knew Christ, we were unable to obey God. God's law was powerless to change us because of our sinful nature. We were enslaved by sin. But God the Father sent his Son. Through his death and resurrection Jesus has liberated us from the penalty and power of sin. And now God the Father has sent the Spirit of his Son. The Spirit gives us a new power and new desires.

How does the Spirit change us? John Owen says that the Spirit supplies "believers with experience of the truth, reality and excellence of the things believed".[1] And as he does that, he gives us faith to believe the truth and a love for Christ which means we turn from our sin and back to Christ.

Christ's commands become lovely to us as he becomes lovely to us. And it's the Spirit who shows us how lovely Christ is. So, as Jeremiah puts it, his law is written "on our hearts" (Jeremiah 31 v 33).

I was talking recently with a new Christian who said that one of the first things she noticed when she be-

---

1 John Owen, **The Holy Spirit**, abridged and simplified by R. J. K. Law, Banner of Truth, 1998, 106.

came a Christian was that she didn't want to use bad language anymore. Before, she'd sworn like a trooper. But when the Spirit made his home in her, she wanted to use her words to honour Christ and to point people to him.

When I was growing up, I had a little Jack Russell dog called Remmy. He was white all over with one brown ear and I loved him. But one day it snowed. And when I let him out into the garden I noticed that he wasn't white at all. My parents both smoked. And over the years my beautiful dog had been stained a horrible nicotine-yellow colour. I'd never noticed before. But now, against the pure-white snow, the staining became obvious.

It's the same with our sin. As we see how glorious Jesus is, so we see our sin more clearly. And we don't like what we see. Things that were OK to us before start to seem horrible. If you've ever felt conviction of sin as you read the Bible or heard it taught, that was the Spirit's work. This means that, even as you're growing in holiness, you may actually feel as if the opposite is happening: the more the Spirit reveals Christ to you, the more you feel uncomfortable about your sin and disgusted by it.

We used to believe the lies of sin. But now the Spirit opens our eyes to the glory of Christ. We begin to recognise by faith that God offers more than sin does. We grow in holiness as we turn from the lies of sin and instead believe the truth about Christ. We grow as we turn from our selfish desires and instead worship Christ. This is the work of the Spirit: showing us the truth about Christ and making Christ desirable to us, more desirable than temptation. John Owen says this: "This is the great work of the Holy Spirit towards the church. He makes Christ glorious in our eyes."[1]

What might this look like in practice?

As Susan reads God's word, the Spirit impresses something amazing on her heart. She doesn't have to live for the approval of her demanding boss, because she's already loved and accepted by Jesus because of the cross. She can relax and get on serving at work.

As Ian sings worship songs with his church, the Spirit brings home to him a truth he's never taken to heart before. Jesus is in control of everything, even his job-hunting. So he doesn't have to panic about his rent. He can rest in his Saviour's sovereignty.

How will I change so that I can patiently parent my kids, even when they trash our local supermarket? Only as the Spirit helps me believe I'm not justified by having well-behaved children, but by Jesus' finished work on the cross. And only as he helps me to treasure Christ more than other people's opinion of me.

In Galatians 5 v 16 Paul says that *if we live by the Spirit, we won't gratify the desires of our sinful natures.* He's not issuing a command. He's making a wonderful promise. As the Spirit leads you to Christ, he'll give you new desires, desires that lead to the fruit of the Spirit in your life: "love, joy, peace, patience, kindness, goodness, faithfulness, gentleness and self-control." (Galatians 5 v 22-23)

---

1 John Owen, **The Holy Spirit,** abridged and simplified by R. J. K. Law, Banner of Truth, 1998, 36.

As the Spirit leads you to Christ, so you start to live like Christ.

- *As the Spirit leads him to Christ, the person addicted to porn begins to find that he's captivated by a better vision—a vision of Christ in all his glory and love. And so he begins to experience the fruit of self-control in his life.*
- *As the Spirit leads her to Christ, the person who struggles with back-biting begins to find she doesn't need to put others down because she has all she needs in Christ. And so she begins to use her words to love those around her.*
- *As the Spirit leads him to Christ, the lazy person begins to see his desires changing. He wants to serve a God like Jesus with every ounce of his energy. And so the fruit of faithfulness begins to appear in his life.*
- *As the Spirit leads her to Christ, the person who's scared to witness to her friends begins to find her heart emboldened to speak of the glory of Christ. Her joy just overflows in evangelism.*
- *And as the Spirit leads him to Christ, the person who gets angry with his children begins to be patient with them as he's overwhelmed by God's patient, loving care for his children in Christ.*

Sometimes change can appear slow. John Owen says this:

> *The growth of trees and plants takes place so slowly that it is not easily seen. Daily we notice little change. But, in the course of time, we see that a great change has taken place. So it is with grace. Sanctification is a progressive, lifelong work.*[1]

Our role is to "keep in step with the Spirit" (Galatians 5 v 25). We're to follow the Spirit's promptings towards holiness. We're to plunder God's word for the treasures of Christ so he's our surpassing delight. We're to surround ourselves with people who speak and sing the gospel to us (Ephesians 5 v 18-19). We're to use the Spirit's power to kill off any hint of sin in our life (Romans 8 v 12-13). If we do these things, we'll be going with the grain of the Spirit's purpose in our lives and not against it.

Philippians 1 v 6 says that:

> he who began a good work in you will carry it on to completion until the day of Christ Jesus.

There may be times when you seem to be going backwards. There may be times when you fall into sin and despair. But have confidence; the Spirit will complete his work in you. Why? Because God has promised it and because the Spirit loves to bring glory to Christ.

---

1 John Owen, **The Holy Spirit**, abridged and simplified by R. J. K. Law, Banner of Truth, 1998, 108-109.

Chapter 3

The Spirit of love

Do you ever find yourself spontaneously crying out to your heavenly Father? Maybe you find yourself sinning again in that same old way. Maybe you hear of a brother or sister in Christ struggling. Maybe you see a breath-taking view. Maybe you hear of someone for whom you've been praying for years becoming a Christian. Or maybe you hear of a dreadful tragedy on the news. And all you can do is cry out, whether in joy or despair, "Father!"

That's the work of the Spirit. When you cry out, "Father!" the Spirit is witnessing to you that you're a child of God. It's not just the moments of joy either. Those moments when you feel most lost and at sea—when all you can do is cry out—are actually moments when the Father is drawing you to himself by the Spirit, and enfolding you in his embrace.

1. The divine family

What do you think of when you think of God? Many

people think of God as a cold, distant, aloof being or force. He's the Creator, but when he lit the fuse of the big bang, he retreated to a safe distance. In contrast, Christians believe God is intimately involved in the world. But many Christians start by thinking of God as a ruler, a ruler whom I'm bound to disappoint. It's certainly true that God is King. But if that's your starting point, then, while you might respect such a God, you're not going to love him. We can end up thinking of God as a lonely, old man who doesn't like being disturbed.

But before God was Creator and before he was King he was a Father. God became the Creator and King when he created the world. But throughout all eternity God has been a Trinity of persons-in-relationship, an eternal family, a community of love. The Father loved the Son before the creation of the world (John 17 v 3) and the Son loves the Father (John 14 v 31). The Father is in the Son and the Son is in the Father (John 17 v 21). The Father sends the Son and the Father gives glory to the Son (John 17 v 21). The Son brings glory to the Father (John 17 v 4). He knows the Father (17 v 25) and petitions the Father (14 v 15). The Son "is in the bosom of the Father" (John 1 v 18 NASB). The Son and the Father have the most loving, intimate relationship possible.

But what about the Spirit? Is he the divine equivalent of an unwanted third person on a date? Not at all! The Spirit shares in their love. At Jesus' baptism, the Father declares his love for the Son: "You are my Son whom I love; with you I am well pleased" (Mark 1 v 11). But what has happened to Jesus just a moment before? We have seen heaven opened and "the Spirit descending on him like a dove" (Mark 1 v 10). As Mike Reeves puts it:

> *The Father declares his love for his Son, and his pleasure in him, and he does so as the Spirit rests on Jesus. For the way the Father makes known his love is precisely through giving his Spirit ... It is all deeply personal: the Spirit stirs up the delight of the Father in the Son and the delight of the Son in the Father, inflaming their love and so binding them together "in the fellowship of the Holy Spirit" (2 Corinthians 13 v 14).*

The Spirit will come in the name of Jesus as the representative of Jesus (John 14 v 26). He is "another" advocate or comforter (John 14 v 16). Just as Jesus was among his disciples—loving them, serving them and teaching them—so the Spirit will continue that ministry among them. In fact, the Spirit, the Son and the Father are so inseparably intertwined that when Jesus tells the disciples of the coming of the Spirit, he says: "I will come to you" (John 14 v 18). And when he talks of the Spirit coming to live in the disciples, he says: "My Father will love [those who obey my teaching], and we will come to them and make our home with them" (John 14 v 23).

At the heart of God is a relationship of love between the Father, the Son and the Spirit. So much so that John can tell us that "God is love" (1 John 4 v 16).

Is the Spirit a person or a force?

The Spirit is described in the Bible as the presence of God, or the way he works. In the NT the Spirit is referred to without an article. Jesus, for example, literally says, "Receive holy spirit," in John 20 v 22. So "Spirit" and "breath" might just be metaphorical descriptions of God's power or God's presence (much as I might say: "I'll be with you in spirit"). Is the Spirit just a way of talking about God-in-action or God-among-us?

In the Old Testament the Spirit or breath of God is used to describe the way God works (Isaiah 40 v 7; Zechariah 4 v 6). But the Spirit is also distinguished from God (Genesis 1 v 2; Numbers 11 v 25; Psalm 104 v 30). The Spirit isn't just a force. He is at work himself.

We find a similar picture in the New Testament. The Spirit is identified with both the Father and the Son. He is the Spirit of God (Romans 8 v 9, 11; 2 Corinthians 3 v 3; 1 John 4 v 2) and the Spirit of Jesus (Acts 16 v 7; Romans 8 v 9; Galatians 4 v 6; Philippians 1 v 19; see also 2 Corinthians 3 v 17-18). To lie to the Spirit is to lie to God (Acts 5 v 3-4). Jesus is present with the disciples through the Spirit (John 14 v 18,23). The Spirit doesn't draw attention to himself. His work is "to the Father" and "to the Son" (Ephesians 2 v 17). He brings the presence of Christ among his people (John 14 v 16-18) and brings glory to the Son (John 16 v 14).

But the Spirit also has a distinct identity from the Father and the Son (Mark 1 v 12; 13 v 11; Luke 4 v 1-2). As Jesus is baptised and as the Father speaks from heaven, the Spirit descends on Jesus in the form of a dove (Matthew 3 v 16-17; Mark 1 v 9-11; Luke 3 v 21-22). The Spirit listens to the Father just as Jesus does (John 16 v 13). He forbids the apostles to preach in Asia (Acts 16 v 6) and warns Paul of the sufferings that await him (Acts 20 v 23). The Spirit has a "mind" (Romans 8 v 27). Christians are to be led by the Spirit (Romans 8 v 14; Galatians 5:18). The Spirit is distinguished from the Father and the Son. He is sent by the Father (John 14 v 16, 26; Galatians 4 v 6) and he is sent by Jesus (John 15 v 26). When Jesus returns to the Father, the Spirit will replace him (John 16 v 7).

The New Testament also makes it clear that the Spirit is a person. In Greek the word "Spirit" is neuter. It should be referred to as "it". But most of the time the New Testament talks about the Holy Spirit as "he" (John 14 v 26; 15 v 26; 16 v 8, 14). Jesus talks of him as the *Paraclete*—a Greek word that combines the ideas of "advocate" and "comforter" (John 14 v 16,26). Jesus says the Spirit is "another Comforter" (John 14 v 16, KJV). In other words, he is a Comforter in the same way Jesus was a Comforter. The Spirit says "for me" and "I" when he calls the church leaders in Antioch to set aside Paul and Barnabas (Acts 13 v 2). Paul warns against "grieving" the Holy Spirit (Ephesians 4 v 30). People can speak or blaspheme against or lie to the Holy Spirit (Matthew 12 v 32; Mark 3 v 28-29; Acts 5 v 1-11).

So the Spirit is a person who is both identified with God and distinguished from the Father and the Son. What does this mean for us?

- The Spirit is God so God himself is present with us.
- The Spirit is not the Father or the Son so the Spirit can make Jesus present in us, even though Jesus is in heaven
- The Spirit is a person so God is personally present with us.

2. Drawn into the divine family

The Trinity isn't a private, holy huddle. The divine family welcomes us in.

Recently, there were huge floods in the town where I live. It rained for two days without stopping. The river burst its banks, water poured into homes, fields were submerged and huge bales of hay were swept away. There was just too much water for the river to hold so it simply had to run over.

In the gospel, God's love has flooded out. The love of the Father, Son and Spirit is not a selfish, introverted love. God is not like those couples who get married and then disappear from society. The Father delights to share his love. In his love for his Son, he delights to see his Son loved by others. There's a deluge of love that overflows to welcome in those who deserve only his wrath. Through the work of the Son and the Spirit, we are drawn into the loving relationships of Father, Son and Spirit. "I will not leave you as orphans," says Jesus to his disciples in John 14 v 18. "I will come to you." And he comes to us by the Spirit.

Before Jesus came and made his home in you by the Spirit, you were an orphan, without hope and without God in the world (Ephesians 2 v 12). But now, because of the Spirit's work in you, you're no longer an orphan. You're a child loved by the heavenly Father. Because the Spirit lives in you, you're in Christ and Christ is in you. And because Christ is in the Father, you're part of the divine family.

The extraordinary fact is this: *the Father loves you with the same love with which he loves his Son, Jesus.* Jesus prays for us: "May they be brought to complete unity to let the world know that you sent me and have loved them even as you have loved me" (John 17 v 23).

If you're trusting Jesus today, then you could not be more loved by the Father than you are right now. You're as *loved* as Jesus, and as *secure* as Jesus. Through the Holy Spirit you have the same intimate relationship with God the Father that Jesus himself has had for all eternity.

3. The Spirit makes us feel part of the divine family

> But when the set time had fully come, God sent his Son, born of a woman, born under the law, to redeem those under the law, that we might receive adoption to sonship. Because you are his sons, God sent the Spirit of his Son into our hearts, the Spirit who calls out, "*Abba*, Father." So you are no longer a slave, but God's child; and since you are his child, God has made you also an heir.
>
> *Galatians 4 v 4-7*

Salvation is a legal act. Jesus meets all the legal requirements for our justification through his death and resurrection. When our friends adopted a child, there was a day when they went to court and the court declared that the child was legally their son. "God sent his Son ... to redeem those under the law, that we might receive the full rights of sons." (v 4-5). Our papers have come through: we are legally the children of God.

But God doesn't just want you to *be* his child. He wants you to *know* you're a child, to *feel it*, to experience his fatherly love and closeness. He sent his Son so we could be his children. He sent "the Spirit of his Son" so we could know we are his children. "Because you are sons, God sent the Spirit of his Son into our hearts" (v 6).

Russell Moore tells the story of how he and his wife adopted two boys from a Russian orphanage:

> *When my wife Maria and I at long last received the call that the legal process was over, and we returned to Russia to pick up our new sons, we found that their transition from orphanage to family was more difficult than we had supposed. We dressed the boys in outfits our parents had bought for them. We nodded our thanks to the orphanage personnel and walked out into the sunlight, to the terror of the two boys.*
>
> *They'd never seen the sun, and they'd never felt the wind. They had never heard the sound of a car door slamming or had the sensation of being carried along at 100 miles an hour down a road. I noticed that they were shaking, and reaching back to the orphanage in the distance.*
>
> *I whispered to Sergei, now Timothy, "That place is a pit! If only you knew what's waiting for you: a home with a Mommy and a Daddy who love you, grandparents and great-grandparents and cousins and playmates and McDonald's Happy Meals!"*
>
> *But all they knew was the orphanage. It was squalid, but they had no other reference point. It was home.*

> *We knew the boys had acclimated to our home, that they trusted us, when they stopped hiding food in their high-chairs. They knew there would be another meal coming, and they wouldn't have to fight for the scraps. This was the new normal.*[1]

"Reaching back to the orphanage." The boys had a wonderful new life. But they didn't realise it yet, and so they were reaching back to the orphanage. We have a wonderful new life as children of God. But when we lose sight of that truth, we reach back to the old life. We worry, we hide food in our high chairs, because we don't yet trust our new Father. Or we reach back to our old sinful ways because we don't yet grasp the privileges and joys of being a child of God.

God wants us to stop reaching back. So he gives us the Holy Spirit. He wants us to stop worrying, stop hiding, stop living like slaves and to enjoy his love. The Spirit is the Spirit of the Son. He gives us a Son-like experience. He helps us experience the same security and affection that the divine Son receives from the Father.

The Father doesn't want your duty. He wants your love. He doesn't want you to act like an employee who discharges his responsibilities. He wants you to live as a royal Son. He wants you to live as a Princess. And so he gives you the Spirit of his Son.

What does this look like? Paul tells us: "Because you are his sons, God sent the Spirit of his Son into our

---

1 Russell Moore, **Adopted for Life**, Crossway, 2009, 43-44.

hearts, the Spirit who calls out, "*Abba*, Father"." (Galatians 4 v 6) Paul says much the same thing in Romans 8 v 15-16:

> The Spirit you received does not make you slaves, so that you live in fear again; rather, the Spirit you received brought about your adoption to sonship. And by him we cry, "*Abba*, Father." The Spirit himself testifies with our spirit that we are God's children.

If you've ever felt the desire to pray to your heavenly Father, that's because the Spirit put that desire in your heart. If you've ever felt that prayer was more than words hitting the ceiling, that's because the Spirit has assured you that you're a child of God. If you've ever gasped: "Thank you, Father!" as you've seen friends responding to the gospel or Christians growing in their relationship with Jesus, that's the Spirit reminding you of your glorious status in Christ. If you love God, that love for God is there because the Spirit put it there. It didn't start with you—by nature we're enemies of God. Your love for God is a sure sign of his love for you.

Romans 5 v 5 tells us: "We know how dearly God loves us, because he has given us the Holy Spirit to fill our hearts with his love" (NLT). And if you've ever cried out: "Father!" in moments of desperation or need, that's the Spirit testifying to your heart that you have a Father who listens to your concerns and cares for your needs.

As I, Chris, was writing this book, my mother died. She was one of my best friends and her witness to me through the tough times of her life was one of the key means of grace God used to bring me to faith in Jesus. One of her last text messages to me from hospital read: "Night, night, my son, brother and co-heir." It's been a painful time. In the moments of intense sadness and loss, sometimes all I've been able to do is cry out: "Father!" And yet it's been a huge encouragement to me to know that, as I do that, it's not just me striving with my strength to reach out to my heavenly Father. Quite the opposite. As I cry out: "Father!", it's the Father himself who is reaching out to me through the Spirit, reminding me that in Jesus I'm his beloved child, and drawing me back into his embrace.

Feelings?

The Spirit's work in us doesn't necessarily lead to a feeling of serenity or calm. There's not always a gushing emotional experience as you praise God—though you might feel that. The word translated "call out" or "cry" in Galatians 4 v 6 and Romans 8 v 15 is a strong word. It's the cry a child makes when she's fallen, when a dog bites, when she's lost. It's the kind of cry that makes a father come running. The phrase "*Abba*, Father" is only used one other time in the New Testament: on the lips of Jesus in Gethsemane when he sweats blood as he faces the prospect of the cross. "*Abba*, Father" is not just about kisses and cuddles.

My (Tim's) 19-year-old daughter was looking after a friend's child recently. I was working upstairs when I heard a plaintive, undulating shout: "Daaaad!" It was a tone of voice I hadn't heard for many years. I ran downstairs to find our two-year-old friend had vomited all over Katie. My independent-minded 19-year-old doesn't normally think she needs her dad. But in this situation she was desperate for my help! It's that cry for help to a father that Paul's talking about.

Russell Moore describes how he was struck by the terrible, poignant silence of the Russian orphanage. Children learn not to cry out when no-one comes to them, when no-one cares for them. For a week Russell Moore and his wife played with their two future sons. They read to them, sang to them, held them loved them. And each evening they walked out, leaving this eerie silence behind. And then on the last day the time came for them to go. They had to go back to the United States to complete the legal formalities before the boys could become part of their family. And Russell Moore says he felt compelled to turn back. He went back in and, quoting the words of Jesus, said: "We will not leave you orphans. We will come for you." And as they walked out down the corridor, they heard one of their sons scream out. The scream of a one-year-old: wordless, angry, desperate. And Russell Moore says it was the most terrible and lovely thing he ever heard. It cut him to the heart, but it was the cry of a son for his father. With that cry of anguish this orphan had become a son.[1]

Adoption is not a sentimental notion. In the brokenness of life the Spirit prompts us to cry out: "Abba, Father." It's the cry of a daughter in Haiti as she sobs with

---

1 Russell Moore, 'Adoption and the Renewal of Creation,' Together For Adoption Conference 2009, togetherforadoption.org, 4'42"-9'25".

a wounded child in her arms in a city in ruins. It's the cry of a son as he feels the pain of a brother walking away from the family. It's the cry of every child of God who calls on God to bring an end to the brokenness of this world.

We call out to God because we know we have a Father. Even when he doesn't feel close, we know he's there and he's listening. Even when we can't find any words to say, the Spirit intercedes on our behalf.

> In the same way, the Spirit helps us in our weakness. We do not know what we ought to pray for, but the Spirit himself intercedes for us through wordless groans.
>
> *Romans 8 v 26*

Listening to the Spirit

But it's possible to grow less aware or less sensitive to the Spirit's prompting in our hearts. It's possible to find ourselves acting more like God's employees than his children. That's what's happened to the Galatians. They've lost their joy (4 v 15). Why? Because they've been duped into thinking they have to earn their relationship with God. They're going back to law (4 v 8-11). They're becoming deaf to the Spirit.

Sometimes I put music on in my study to drown out noises in the rest of the house so I'm not distracted as I work. Every day there are noises that distract us from intimacy with our Father. The cry of the world, telling us we need the things it's offering to be truly happy. The cry of sin, telling us we're too guilty to be called God's child. The cry of law, telling us we have to perform if we want to know the Father's favour.

We need to push aside these voices and tune our hearts to the prompting of the Spirit. We need to ask the Spirit to help us enjoy the full freedom of being beloved children of the Father. We need to read the Bible asking the Spirit to speak to us through it. Galatians 4 v 4-7 would be a great place to start. Memorise these words so you can put them on like headphones to block out the distracting noise of the false voices in the world around us.

During the last few days of my mother's life, she was struggling to breathe. We'd been reading Romans 8 v 15-17—one of her favourite passages. As she breathed in, gasping for air, she would mouth the word: "*Abba!*" And as she breathed out she would whisper, "Father!" The intensive-care unit was full of machines bleeping, nurses hustling round, patients being moved about. Death and sickness were all around her. But there she was, a dependent child, calling out to her Father, the Spirit reminding her that she was safe in Christ. And so she died, looking forward to the fullness of what she'd experienced, knowing that she was a dearly loved child of her Father. And that is the work of the Spirit.

Should we pray to the Spirit?

The normal pattern for prayer in the New Testament is that we pray *to* the Father *through* the Son *with the help of* the Holy Spirit. But Jesus and the Holy Spirit are both God and so we can pray to both.

So our normal practice should be to pray to the Father (with an awareness of the Son's mediation and the Spirit's help). But it can also be helpful sometimes to pray to the Spirit to affirm the distinctive role he plays in our lives and to raise our expectations of his work.

Chapter 4

The Spirit of truth

Jane was annoyed. She'd been struggling to work out what to do about her job for ages. Her hours had been getting out of hand and the travelling was leaving her exhausted. She was hardly ever at mid-week church get-togethers these days.

On the other hand, she'd had some great opportunities to share her faith with people at work. She'd been asking God for wisdom, but she still felt no clearer. She'd even spoken with some friends for advice, but they'd just asked her what she thought God was saying to her about it. And that's what annoyed her—they were just being way too super-spiritual. God doesn't speak to you like that today, does he?

1. The Spirit has spoken

Jesus makes a startling promise in John 16 v 13-14:

> When he, the Spirit of truth, comes, he will guide you into all the truth. He will not speak on his

own; he will speak only what he hears, and he will tell you what is yet to come. He will glorify me because it is from me that he will receive what he will make known to you.

Who is that promise for?

In one sense it's for all believers. The Spirit guides believers into all truth, revealing God's glory and making Christ known to us. But in another sense this is a promise with special meaning for the first disciples. Jesus is promising that the Holy Spirit will help them (and those under their supervision) to write an authoritative account about Jesus. The Spirit will give them everything they need to write the New Testament.

So why did John include this in his Gospel? Why is it important for us to hear this promise that Jesus made to the apostles? Because Jesus wanted us to be confident that the New Testament is not just a collection of personal memoirs, but the Holy Spirit's own account of who Jesus is and what he came to do.

Jesus is God's "Word" (John 1 v 1-2). He is God revealing himself to us in all his glory. And the New Testament is the Spirit's witness to that Word. As the New Testament writers wrote the story of Jesus in the Gospels and explained that story in the letters, the Holy Spirit was guiding them "into all the truth". As a result we can have complete confidence that every word of the New Testament is God's own witness about Jesus, the Word made flesh.

The same is true of the Old Testament. Hebrews introduces one of David's psalms with the words: "As the

Holy Spirit says" (Hebrews 3 v 7). The whole Bible was written through the Holy Spirit. Paul says in 2 Timothy 3 v 16-17: "All Scripture is God-breathed". The Greek word for "Spirit" and "breath" are the same. So Paul is saying that the whole of the Old Testament was "Spirited" out by God! The result is the Bible. In the Bible God the Father reveals himself in his Son through the Holy Spirit. So we can have complete confidence when we read the Bible that we are hearing the voice of God.

The Spirit has spoken every part of Scripture

Paul says: "All Scripture is God-breathed and is useful for teaching" (2 Timothy 3 v 16). Every part of it—even those bits like Paul's request to Timothy to bring his cloak (2 Timothy 4 v 13). It's not just Jesus' words that are God speaking to us (as some red-letter versions of the Bible seem to suggest). Every part of Scripture is the word of Christ spoken through the Spirit. There are different kinds of literature which need to be handled differently, but all of it was breathed out by God through the Spirit.

The Spirit has spoken every word of Scripture

Some people have claimed that the truths of Scripture are inspired by the Spirit, but not the actual words. But that's not what the Bible says about itself. The Bible ends with a warning not to meddle with any of the words of Scripture (Revelation 22 v 18-19). We can't pick and choose which bits of Scripture we like. Every word is an authoritative word from God.

The Spirit has spoken through human authors

Hebrews 3 v 7 says the Holy Spirit spoke the words of Psalm 95. Then in 4 v 7 the writer says it was David who wrote the psalm. So did David or the Spirit write Psalm 95?

The answer is *both*.

The Bible was written by human authors, but the Spirit ensured that what they wrote is the very word of God. They didn't write in a trance. We see their personalities and individual styles. Yet they "spoke from God as they were carried along by the Holy Spirit" (2 Peter 1 v 21).

Over 40 authors with different personalities wrote 66 different books in very different cultures over a period of about 1,500 years, using many different kinds of literature. Yet what they wrote consistently tells one big story: the story of Jesus Christ, the world's Saviour and King. How is that possible? Because the Spirit of Truth was speaking through each one.

The Spirit has spoken and the result is the Bible—God's final, authoritative word about Jesus, the Word made flesh.

2. The Spirit speaks today

So the Spirit ensures the revelation of God was spoken in the Bible. But that's not enough. He needed to work in the hearts of the human writers to ensure that what they wrote was God's word. But he also needs to work in the hearts of readers to ensure that we hear what they wrote as God's word. The objective revelation of God is not enough because our hearts are deaf to God's word.

Left to ourselves, we block out the voice of God in our lives.

> The person without the Spirit does not accept the things that come from the Spirit of God but considers them foolishness, and cannot understand them because they are discerned only through the Spirit." *1 Corinthians 2 v 14*

But in his grace, God gave us the Spirit so that we can receive his word as the very words of God.

> For who knows a person's thoughts except their own spirit within them? In the same way no one knows the thoughts of God except the Spirit of God. What we have received is not the spirit of the world, but the Spirit who is from God, so that we may understand what God has freely given us.
> *1 Corinthians 2 v 11-12*

It's not just that the Spirit helps us understand what God spoke in the past. That's amazing enough. But there's more. Hebrews 3 v 7 introduces its quote from Psalm 95 with the words: "So, as the Holy Spirit says: 'Today, if you hear his voice...'" Did you notice which tense the writer uses? He uses the present tense. "As the Holy Spirit says." The Spirit has not only spoken. He speaks through God's word today.

If you read an autobiography, you get some insight into the mind of the author. But you can hardly claim to know them or have a relationship with them. In the same way, the Bible is a book about God written by God. But that's not enough to give us a relationship with God. We can only have a relationship with God if he actually speaks to us. Today.

We long for God to tell us that he loves us, to let us in on his plans, to pour out his heart to us, to whisper in our ears. And that is what the Spirit does! The Spirit speaks to us through the Bible. The Bible is not just a collection of stories and facts about God. It's the means the Spirit uses to speak to us and therefore to relate to us. Hebrews 4 v 12-13 says: "The word of God is living and active". It's almost as if you could put it to your ear and hear it pulsing! The word of God comes alive as we read it through the life-giving Spirit.

So if you want to hear from God, get into the Bible. John Calvin says:

> *The Holy Spirit cannot be separated from his truth which he has expressed in Scripture. This means that the Holy Spirit shows his power only when we give Scripture the reverence and dignity that belong to it.*[1]

If you want to experience the power of the Spirit, read the Bible expectantly, hear it taught reliably and use it to encourage one another. And ask the Spirit to speak to you. Don't read the Bible just to learn more about God. Come to Scripture ready to be addressed personally by God. When you're listening to teaching in church, ask

1 John Calvin, **Institutes**, 1.9.3 (my translation).

the Spirit to show you what you need to see about Jesus. When you're reading the Bible on your own, pray: "Holy Spirit, what would you say to me today?"

That doesn't mean we should expect a big, emotional experience every time. But we should expect the Holy Spirit to expose our sin and grow our love for Christ. Why? Because the Spirit loves to bring glory to Christ by taking what is his and making it ours!

3. The Spirit leads

The Old Testament law laid down rules for all sorts of situations. "If this happens, do this," it said. "And if this happens, do this." Exodus 21 v 28, for example, says: "If a bull gores a man or woman to death, the bull is to be stoned to death, and its meat must not be eaten. But the owner of the bull will not be held responsible." Theologians call this casuistic law or case-law. It tells you how you have to behave in a specific situation.

In the New Testament, however, we get very little of this kind of case-law. And that's surprising because the first believers were trying to live with Jesus as Lord in an empire which told them Caesar was Lord. Their lives were full of questions about how to behave in tricky situations. Why isn't there more in the New Testament about how to act in specific circumstances?

Paul gives us a clue in Romans 12 v 1-3:

> Therefore, I urge you, brothers and sisters, in view of God's mercy, to offer your bodies as a living sacrifice, holy and pleasing to God—this is your true and proper worship. Do not conform to the

pattern of this world, but be transformed by the renewing of your mind. Then you will be able to test and approve what God's will is—his good, pleasing and perfect will.

Paul is urging God's people to live radical lives of service for God. He tells them to "test and approve what God's will is". They're to find out how God wants them to live. But Paul doesn't lay down any case-law for them to help them to do this. Instead he tells them: "Be transformed by the renewing of your mind". They'll learn God's will by having their minds renewed. But how can a Christian have their mind renewed? Titus 3 v 4 tells us that this "renewal" is the work of the Spirit. The Spirit leads God's people.

The Spirit changes our perspective to make us wise

As the Spirit teaches us from God's word, we begin to see the world from God's perspective. We're able to "test and approve what God's will is". We start to see our money in the light of God's generosity, so we're able to make godly decisions about what to do with it. We see our time in the light of God's priorities, so we're able to make godly decisions about how best to use it. This doesn't happen in a single moment. Instead over the course of our lives, the Spirit transforms our minds to see things God's way.

The Spirit guides us in specific situations

In many situations the choices we face are not "right or wrong" choices. Do I spend my time cleaning the house or meeting up with my neighbour? What should I pray for my friend? What should I say in this situation? Sometimes in these situations the Spirit guides us in specific ways.

A few weeks ago my (Chris's) wife, Laura, was taking one of our children to a party on a Saturday afternoon. She'd decided she wouldn't stay at the party because she needed to get things ready for entertaining people that evening. But when she got to the party, she saw that the lady giving the party didn't have many people to help. She felt prompted by the Spirit to lend a hand, even though she had lots of jobs to do back at home. This led to great opportunities to share the gospel with other parents. And when she got home she found I'd been unexpectedly freed up, so I'd been able to get things ready for our guests while she was out at the party.

The Spirit may prompt us to pray for certain things. He may give us a desire to serve in particular ways. He may lead us to speak to certain people, just as he led Philip to speak to the Ethiopian eunuch in Acts 8 v 26-40. Different Christians talk in different ways about this work of the Spirit: "God prompted me." "The Spirit led me." "I received a word of knowledge." "God called me." "As the preacher spoke, I felt God speaking to me." "God brought a verse to mind." "I felt it laid on my heart." "I was given a prophecy." Whatever words we use to describe it, we're often talking about the same thing: the Spirit of God leading the people of God.

What does that mean for us? It doesn't mean that we have to wait for the prompting of the Spirit before we get on with serving Jesus. Sometimes Christians can wait for the Spirit to guide them. But the Spirit has already spoken in the Bible and the Bible gives us all we need to get on with living godly lives for Jesus' glory. It's even more important for us to recognise that the Spirit will never prompt us to do something that goes against what he has already said in Scripture.

But it does mean we should be sensitive to the prompting of the Spirit. "Lord, please show me how to spend my time today." "Show me how to love this person." "How should I pray for this situation?" "What should I say to this person?"

Remember what Jesus said about the Holy Spirit: "He will glorify me because it is from me that he will receive what he will make known to you" (John 16 v 14). The Spirit loves to bring glory to Jesus by taking the truth of Jesus and making it known to us. That's why he spoke God's truth into the Scriptures. That's why he speaks to us today through the Scriptures. And that's why he guides God's people to live lives that bring glory to the Son.

What is the gift of prophecy and is it for today?

The New Testament gift of prophecy is different from Old Testament prophecy. Paul says the church is "built on the foundation of the apostles and prophets" (Ephesians 2 v 20). The equivalent of Old Testament prophecy is the apostolic testimony recorded in the New Testament. Old Testament prophets and New Testament apostles brought God's authoritative word to his people. In contrast, New Testament prophecy is to be weighed and tested (1 Thessalonians 5 v 19-22).

Some people think prophecy no longer exists today. They believe it was replaced by the finished New Testament. Talking about prophecy today is confusing, they suggest, because it might lead people to expect something equivalent to Scripture. Sometimes people cite 1 Corinthians 13 v 8-10, which says prophecy and tongues will cease when "completeness" comes.

Other people see nothing in the New Testament to suggest prophecy will stop. They believe the "completeness" in 1 Corinthians 13 is a reference to the return of Christ. It may be true that we should expect more prophecy where God's word is not readily available (which includes the time before the Bible was finished, but also includes the frontiers of mission today), but God still works through the Spirit to strengthen his church.

A key question is: *What is New Testament prophecy?*

At its heart, prophecy seems to be bringing God's word to bear in a particular situation. So it's intimately tied to God's word in the Bible, but also involves applying that word to specific situations. Paul says we should "eagerly desire gifts of the Spirit, especially prophecy" because "the one who prophesies speaks to people for their strengthening, encouraging and comfort" (1 Corinthians 14 v 1, 3). Sometimes that means predicting the future (as with Agabus in Acts 11 v 27-30). But more generally, prophecy brings the truth to bear on people's hearts so they can be strengthened, encouraged and comforted.

Most New Testament gifts are also duties. There are evangelists, but we're all called to evangelise. The same is true with pastoral care, teaching, exercising faith and so on. In the same way, we're all called to speak "the truth in love" to one another (Ephesians 4 v 11, 15), but some have a particular gift for bringing God's word to bear in the lives of God's people. This is the gift of prophecy.

Sometimes this can happen through preaching when it feels that the preaching is speaking just to you. Perhaps it feels as if the preacher has a special insight into your life at that particular moment in time.

Some people have a particular gift of bringing God's word to bear in an incisive way. They sense the Spirit saying something particular to a person or a church. A friend might say: "I've been praying for you and I wonder if the Lord might be using this problem to teach you ..." Or sometimes in a pastoral situation someone may say something that cuts through the issue someone wants help with to the real issue underneath.

Different church traditions have different ways of talking about these experiences. And some churches are wary of talking about prophecy because it can undermine the authority and sufficiency of the Bible. A big danger is that people start to value the prophecy over Scripture. So, whatever you call it, all of this needs to be tentative. No-one should say: "This is the word of the Lord". Prophecy needs to be tested against Scripture and weighed by church leaders (1 Corinthians 14 v 29).

Chapter 5

The Spirit of power

Mark felt pretty useless. He loved Jesus and he really wanted to be useful to him. And he was excited about the opportunities he had to share Jesus with his workmates. But it was church that got him down. Everyone else in his church seemed so much better at serving Jesus.

John was great at leading Bible studies. Angie was amazing at sharing her faith with anything that had a heart-beat. And Pete could lead sung worship so well. Mark couldn't do any of those things. He knew that Jesus had said to the disciples that his power would come upon his disciples. But Mark just felt so weak. Did he really have the Spirit's power at all?

Jesus promises his disciples:

> **"You will receive power when the Holy Spirit comes on you; and you will be my witnesses in Jerusalem, and in all Judea and Samaria, and to the ends of the earth."** *Acts 1 v 8*

The Christian life is a life of power—power to be Jesus' witnesses to the ends of the earth. And that power comes from the Holy Spirit. What should a life lived in the power of the Spirit look like? And why do we often feel so weak as Christians?

Jesus in the power of the Spirit

Perhaps you think of Jesus as a superhuman who was always capable and totally self-sufficient. But Luke portrays him as utterly dependent on the the Holy Spirit. Jesus was conceived "by the power of Holy Spirit" in the virgin Mary (Luke 1 v 35), and his public ministry didn't begin until the Spirit descends on him at his baptism (Luke 3 v 22).

From his baptism on, Jesus was plunged into this Spirit-empowered work. Luke tells us that "Jesus, full of the Holy Spirit, left the Jordan and was led by the Spirit into the wilderness" (Luke 4 v 1). Jesus then "returned to Galilee in the power of the Spirit" (Luke 4 v 14). He announced the beginning of his public ministry by declaring: "The Spirit of the Lord is on me, because he has anointed me to proclaim good news to the poor" (Luke 4 v 18).

The word "Christ" literally means "anointed One". David was anointed as Israel's king with oil. Jesus was anointed with the Holy Spirit (Isaiah 11 v 2; 61 v 1-2). In Luke 5 v 17 we're told that "the power of the Lord was with Jesus to heal those who were ill". In Luke 10 v 21 Jesus was "full of joy through the Holy Spirit".

Jesus conducted his whole ministry in the power of the Spirit. Luke records how Peter summarised Jesus' ministry:

> "God anointed Jesus of Nazareth with the Holy Spirit and power, and ... he went around doing good and healing all who were under the power of the devil, because God was with him."
>
> *Acts 10 v 38*

Even in his death and resurrection, Jesus was reliant on the Spirit's help:

> How much more, then, will the blood of Christ, who through the eternal Spirit offered himself unblemished to God, cleanse our consciences from acts that lead to death, so that we may serve the living God! *Hebrews 9 v 14*

> [God's Son] who through the Spirit of holiness was appointed the Son of God in power, by his resurrection from the dead: Jesus Christ our Lord.
>
> *Romans 1 v 4*

In all of his earthly ministry, Jesus did nothing except by the power of the Holy Spirit.

Power to be witnesses

When the disciples heard Jesus promise they would receive power when the Holy Spirit came upon them, what did they think this might involve? Perhaps they thought of the individuals in the Old Testament who received God's Spirit to empower them to serve God: people like Moses, Joshua, Samson and David. But perhaps they also thought of the Lord Jesus himself. The

Spirit empowered Jesus to be the Christ, God's King and Saviour. That's not our role! The Spirit doesn't empower us to do that. But the Spirit *does* empower us to fulfil the role God has assigned to us: *to witness to Jesus the Christ.*

The disciples weren't an impressive bunch. They all abandoned Jesus the moment it got tough. Peter denied he even knew his Master when a humble servant-girl accused him of being with Jesus.

Then on the day of Pentecost everything changes. This same Peter addresses a huge crowd of people, showing that Jesus is the promised Christ. As a result 3,000 people are baptised. It's not long before Peter and John are imprisoned and put on trial. We read:

> Then Peter, filled with the Holy Spirit, said to them: "Rulers and elders of the people! ... Salvation is found in no-one else, for there is no other name under heaven given to mankind by which we must be saved." *Acts 4 v 8, 12*

What's happened? The Holy Spirit! God has given his Spirit to empower his people. Now the disciples are filled to bursting with the Spirit of Christ. Christ himself has come to live in them by the Spirit and so now they speak of Christ with a new boldness.

How does the Spirit make timid people so bold? In the same way he does everything he does: by making the truth about Jesus so real to them that they can't stop themselves speaking about him!

But what should I do if I don't feel bold? Prayer is

a great place to start. When the disciples are warned to stop preaching Jesus, they pray for continued boldness. We read:

> After they prayed, the place where they were meeting was shaken. And they were all filled with the Holy Spirit and spoke the word of God boldly.
>
> *Acts 4 v 31*

But what should you do when an opportunity to talk about Jesus arises and you don't feel bold? There's no magic formula. Just start talking and the Spirit will do the rest. We experience the empowering presence of the Spirit as we need it. Jesus says:

> "When you are brought before synagogues, rulers and authorities, do not worry about how you will defend yourselves or what you will say, for the Holy Spirit will teach you at that time what you should say." *Luke 12 v 11-12*

Some of us never experience the Spirit's empowering presence because we avoid situations in which we need to rely on the Spirit's power.

Power to be servants

Maybe you feel that you don't have a role in your church or that other people are much more skilled than you. The Bible says the Spirit empowers each and every Christian to contribute to the life of the church. Here's how Paul puts it in 1 Corinthians 12 v 4-11:

There are different kinds of gifts, but the same Spirit distributes them. There are different kinds of service, but the same Lord. There are different kinds of working, but in all of them and in everyone it is the same God at work. Now to each one the manifestation of the Spirit is given for the common good. To one there is given through the Spirit a message of wisdom, to another a message of knowledge by means of the same Spirit, to another faith by the same Spirit, to another gifts of healing by that one Spirit, to another miraculous powers, to another prophecy, to another distinguishing between spirits, to another speaking in different kinds of tongues, and to still another the interpretation of tongues. All these are the work of one and the same Spirit, and he distributes them to each one, just as he determines.

Your church needs you

Each one of us—including you—has been given "a manifestation of the Spirit" for the good of our church. The Holy Spirit has given you specific skills to use to serve in your church. *And that means your church needs you.*

Paul imagines a body in which a foot sees the dexterity of a hand and says: "Because I am not a hand, I do not belong to the body". Or an ear says: "because I am not an eye, I do not belong to the body". They may not be a hand or eye, but bodies still need feet and ears. "If the whole body were an eye, where would the sense of hearing be? If the whole body were an ear, where would the sense of smell be? But in fact God has arranged the parts of the body, every one of them, just as he wanted them to be." (1 Corinthians 12 v 15-18)

God has equipped his people with different gifts so that they can function together. We're like a body with its different members all working together, or an orchestra with its different instruments playing together to create a rich harmony. Where would the harmony be if they were all first violins? God gave you your abilities because he knew your church would need those abilities.

Should we expect Pentecost to be repeated?

Some people think we should expect Pentecost-like experiences in our lives. Certainly in Acts there are some events that look a lot like Pentecost all over again—in Samaria (Acts 8 v 14-17), Caesarea (Acts 10 v 44-48) and Ephesus (Acts 19 v 1-7).

In the context of the Bible story, it's hard to ignore the *unique* significance of Pentecost. Peter himself explains what happens as the fulfilment of Joel's prophecy of the outpouring of the Spirit on all God's people (Acts 2 v 14-21). Pentecost marks the move from the old covenant to the new covenant, and under the new covenant all God's people experience the Spirit living in them all the time (Jeremiah 31 v 31-34; Ezekiel 36 v 25-27). At Pentecost the disciples became new-covenant believers, with the Holy Spirit not just *operating* on *them* to give them faith, but *living in them* to empower them for mission. From then on, all new believers would receive new birth through the Spirit with the Spirit dwelling in them from the start.

So what are we to make of the experiences in Samaria, Caesarea and Ephesus?

We need to remember that Acts is shaped by the commission of Jesus in Acts 1 v 8: "You will receive power when the Holy Spirit comes on you; and you will be my witnesses in Jerusalem, and in all Judea and Samaria, and to the ends of the earth."

The events in Samaria and Caesarea are the first time the gospel moves into Judea and Samaria and then beyond Palestine to the ends of the earth. These extraordinary outpourings of the Spirit are an echo of Pentecost; they authenticate the move of the gospel outside the bounds of Judaism. This is how Peter explains it in Acts 11 v 15-17. Graham Cole says: "They are Pentecost extended, not Pentecost as paradigm [ie: a patter to be followed]."[1]

The episode in Ephesus is different. There are good reasons to think these people were not Christians at all. They're called "disciples", but they only knew the baptism of John. When Paul hears they've not heard of the Holy Spirit, he preaches Christ (not the Spirit) to them. No doubt he also talked about the Holy Spirit, but he was preaching the gospel to them so they could turn to Christ. When they turned to Christ, then they also at that point received the Holy Spirit.

---

1 Graham A. Cole, **He Who Gives Life: The Doctrine of the Holy Spirit**, Crossway, 2007, 196.

You need your church

This principle of mutual dependence works in both directions. No-one can say they don't need others in the church. Paul says that would be like an eye saying to a hand: "I don't need you!" (1 Corinthians 12 v 21-26). Just because a hand can't see doesn't mean it doesn't have an important role to play. Just because other people can't do what you can do doesn't mean you don't need them. The Holy Spirit has given them abilities that you need in your life and ministry.

A truly spiritual congregation isn't one where a few people exercise spectacular gifts. It's a congregation where the beautiful diversity of the Spirit's gifts to his people is working together. None of us needs feel inferior. None of us can afford to feel superior. We need one another.

Paul gives three different lists of gifts in Romans 12 v 6-8, 1 Corinthians 12 v 7-11 and 1 Corinthians 12 v 27-31. They're all different, so none of them is a definitive list. They include the spectacular and the mundane. Christians sometimes disagree over exactly what is meant by some of these gifts. But that's to miss the point. Paul's point is that a spiritual gift is anything the Spirit uses to build up the church in Christ.

How can I serve my church in the power of the Spirit? None of the lists of the Spirit's gifts in the New Testament comes with an exhortation to individuals to work out what their gifts are and then use those gifts. That's not their point. Their point is that we should appreciate the diversity in the church and not wish we were like someone else or that other people were like us. What we're called to do is serve the body of Christ, asking the Spirit to equip us to be useful.

So look for opportunities to serve. The chances are you'll end up being asked to do things that you're good at (in other words, what the Spirit has gifted you to do). But the important thing for you is to have an attitude of service. So don't say: *I'm not doing that because that's not my gift.* The Spirit's gifts are not given for our personal self-fulfilment, but to build up the body. So building up the body is to be our top concern. And if that means putting out chairs—then put out chairs.

And be encouraged. Have you ever pointed another Christian to a specific Bible passage? Have you every helped another Christian move to a new house or put up a shelf for them or given them a lift? Have you ever looked after someone's children? Have you encouraged someone with the truth of the gospel? All these acts of service show that the Spirit is working in power through you!

Conclusion

Be humble and dependent. If even Jesus was dependent on the Spirit, then how much more must we depend on him. Why did Jesus tell the disciples to wait in Jerusalem until the gift of the Spirit had been given to them (Acts 1 v 4)? Because he knew that without the Spirit working in them, they could do nothing. And neither can we.

Be encouraged and expectant. You may feel weak. You may feel useless. You may not have a clue what spiritual gifts you have or how the Spirit is using you. But be full of courage and expectancy. *Why?* Because the same Spirit who empowered Christ for his ministry is at work in you. So pray with ambition. Expect the Spirit to work through you. The Spirit who loves to bring glory to Christ is living in you to empower you to witness to Christ and to build up his body.

Are miraculous gifts for today?

Some Christians think that the more miraculous gifts such as prophecy, speaking in tongues and healing stopped with the completion of the New Testament. Others believe that those gifts continue unchanged today.

It does seem that, even in the Bible story, signs and wonders were clustered around key people—prophets in the Old Testament like Moses and Elijah, and in the New Testament around the incarnation of Jesus and the initial ministry of his apostles.

These spectacular gifts were given to authenticate the ministry of those men and the words they spoke. So we shouldn't necessarily expect the same level of spectacular miracles today. Indeed, few people today claim to be able to walk on water as Jesus did in Mark 6.

But God is still involved in the lives of his people. He still works miracles. The Spirit loves to reveal Christ to people, so we should pray for healing and for gifts of healing, tongues, interpretation and prophecy.

Other titles in this series

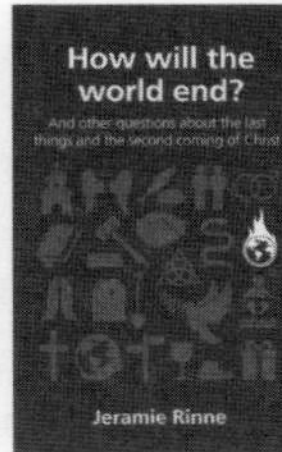

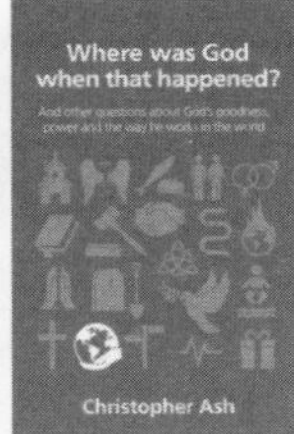

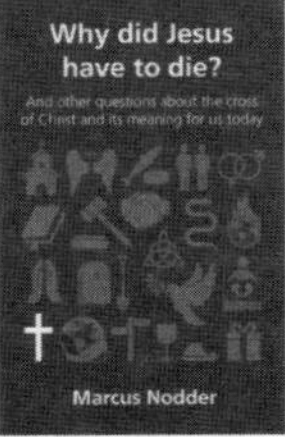

thegoodbook.com | thegoodbook.co.uk
thegoodbook.com.au | thegoodbook.co.nz

BIBLICAL | RELEVANT | ACCESSIBLE

At The Good Book Company, we are dedicated to helping Christians and local churches grow. We believe that God's growth process always starts with hearing clearly what he has said to us through his timeless word—the Bible.

Ever since we opened our doors in 1991, we have been striving to produce resources that honour God in the way the Bible is used. We have grown to become an international provider of user-friendly resources to the Christian community, with believers of all backgrounds and denominations using our Bible studies, books, evangelistic resources, DVD-based courses and training events.

We want to equip ordinary Christians to live for Christ day by day, and churches to grow in their knowledge of God, their love for one another, and the effectiveness of their outreach.

Call us for a discussion of your needs or visit one of our local websites for more information on the resources and services we provide.

Your friends at The Good Book Company
